Welcome to the "Last Frontier!" This sign was originally photographed in 1993 along the road just as one drove across the bridge over the Barron River heading into Everglades City. Unfortunately, the sign disappeared and has not been seen in over two decades. (Photograph by author.)

ON THE COVER: Pictured is a group shot of the laborers who worked on the Tamiami Trail road construction from 1923 to 1928. The two women at right (in white) worked in the mobile dining/mess halls, which were operational around the clock. (Courtesy of Collier County Museum.).

IMAGES of America
EVERGLADES CITY

Maureen Sullivan-Hartung

Copyright © 2020 by Maureen Sullivan-Hartung
ISBN 978-1-4671-0572-9

Published by Arcadia Publishing
Charleston, South Carolina

Printed in the United States of America

Library of Congress Control Number: 2020937636

For all general information, please contact Arcadia Publishing:
Telephone 843-853-2070
Fax 843-853-0044
E-mail sales@arcadiapublishing.com
For customer service and orders:
Toll-Free 1-888-313-2665

Visit us on the Internet at www.arcadiapublishing.com

CONTENTS

Acknowledgments		6
Introduction		7
1.	Who Was Barron Gift Collier?	9
2.	Constructing Tamiami Trail with Blood, Sweat, and Mosquitoes	17
3.	Creating the Company Town of Everglades	43
4.	Plume Hunting, Moonshine, and Square Grouper	63
5.	Inspiring Pioneer Women of the Everglades	75
6.	Historically Significant	83
7.	Neighboring Chokoloskee Island	91
8.	The Town of Ochopee	105
9.	Visiting Copeland, Deep Lake, and Lee Cypress	111
10.	A Giant Passes	125
About the Author		127

Acknowledgments

My first thank-you goes to my mother, Joyce Templin Sullivan, who instilled in me the love of reading. She passed just prior to my deadline submission.

Barron Gift Collier certainly earns both my admiration and thanks for providing me with the story of our county's early history to enjoy and share with others.

To my dear husband, Phillip, who still loves me after everything I have put him through these past 29 years, including two books in the past 10 years; thank you for everything.

The following have enabled me to complete this book, and I thank every one of you from the bottom of my heart: Arcadia Publishing staff; Aunt Joan Templin Haeberle, to whom I am forever indebted; Avis Cooper; Barbara Hinkson, a previous fan and longtime special friend; Bree Cameron, my sweet niece and consummate cheerleader from afar; Big Cypress National Preserve; Collier County Museum; Dick Jay, talented local artist and fisherman; Everglades City; Florida Southern College; fans Gail and Tom Merkle; Ginny Atchison, my computer whiz, who has made this book possible; Glenda Hancock, my No. 1 local historian; HistoryMiami Museum; HITEK Imaging; J.B. Singletary, fellow historian; Jeanie Smith; Jeff Whichello, fellow author; Judy Oxtoby; Lila Zuck, longtime friend, cheerleader, and local history buff as well as author of several local history books; Lynda (Trailways) Little and her amazing aunt; Marney Reed, former Everglades boat captain; Martha Hutcheson, soaring in the skies these days; Naples Historical Society, Inc.; forever friends Paula and Tom Falciglia; best friend ever Prissy Jay (gone but not forgotten); Robert S. Carr, fellow author; Ron Echols, fellow historian; Rookery Bay Estuarine Research Reserve; Scott Salley, longtime friend from day one in Naples; State Archives of Florida; Tim McBride, fellow author; Timothy Harrington, fellow author; Capt. Thomas B. Smith, from the Collier County Sheriff's Office Alumni Association; my late colorful friend and fellow author Totch Brown; Thomas Lockyear; Wayne Maynard, grandson of Collier County's first sheriff; and all of these incredible people within these pages who came before us to make our lives so much richer due to their tenacity and perseverance, we salute you. And to my sisters Annette, Kim, Colleen, and Bettina.

Any mistakes are mine.

Introduction

This Everglade region, from the late 1880s, was a remote and untamed wilderness. A few hardy souls would venture to Southwest Florida, including both John Weeks and William Smith Allen. Both men are believed to have been this area's first permanent residents before later moving on. Allen did not particularly care for the remoteness and sold his holdings to newcomer George Storter Jr. in 1889 for $800.

Enter Barron Gift Collier, a self-made streetcar advertising millionaire, originally from Tennessee, a man with a vision and a dream to create a town where people would want to live. This untouched and untamed wilderness, with its less than 12 families, fascinated Collier and ultimately served as the "hub" of his Southwest Florida empire.

Within two years of his arrival to Everglade in 1921, he would add an 's' to the town's name, after promising the Florida State Legislature to complete the stymied Tamiami Trail road project using his own funds in exchange for the creation of Collier County from a portion of southern Lee County. On May 8, 1923, lawmakers signed the new county into law.

Collier immediately began to work on completing the Tamiami Trail project, which would take five years, from 1923 to 1928. Simultaneously, Collier was creating his vision of a "company town," four miles from the trail's entrance. His first order of business was to hire a manager for these various projects. He met his match and hired David Graham Copeland, a recent US Naval Academy graduate who was up for the challenge. Copeland was meticulous as Collier's chief engineer while keeping Collier's varied projects in check.

In addition to the Tamiami Trail road construction project, Collier knew he would need protection for those travelers riding along on the wide-open roadway once completed, and he decided to hire six couples to man the six way stations he planned to construct, approximately 10 miles apart along the trail from East Naples over to the Miami-Dade County line. These couples lived in the station, on the second floor, and while the wife operated the station, offering light refreshments and pumping gasoline on the premises, her husband became part of the Southwest Mounted Police, later inducted into the Collier County Sheriff's Office. The men were issued a Harley Davidson motorcycle and a smart uniform, based on the fashion style of the Canadian County Mounties, and they would traverse the trail between their own station and the next one up the road while providing assistance running the gamut of flat tires to shoveling dead animals from the road since there were still many wild animals roaming this area. Remember, there were no streetlights or even residential homes or businesses along this stretch of road from 1928 through roughly 1934, when Collier disbanded the stations.

Meanwhile, back in the company town, Collier announced his plan for development in Florida's swamp and wilderness. Collier wanted those living here to have local access to a bank, grocery, movie theater, two-room schoolhouse, clinic, shops, hotel with a restaurant, laundry facilities, and a weekly newspaper—the *Collier County News*. In addition to both water and electricity, steady mail service, telegraphs, and telephones were established; the latter service especially for Collier so he could stay in touch with his company, Collier's Consolidated Street Railway Advertising Company, in New York City. Copeland was up to the task of developing Collier's company town with military precision. It was said that Collier's Inter-County Telegraph & Telephone Company, a 13-county network, would eventually grow into the United Telephone Company.

Collier had boundless energy and normally worked 12-hour days. In addition to his work in Southwest Florida, Collier also served as a special deputy commissioner for public safety in New York. He is credited with the white and yellow divider lines on highways. Collier was a founding member of INTERPOL, the international world police. He was also both interested and instrumental in the national Boy Scout movement.

Upon his sudden death in 1939, Collier was listed as Florida's largest landowner. Unfortunately, he passed before seeing many of his dreams come to fruition. Collier was a man who would not only rub shoulders with presidents and foreign dignitaries, but also other business magnates as well as the common man working construction on his Tamiami Trail road crew or a laborer from his 4C's grapefruit canning company in nearby Deep Lake. Collier was at home in any given situation but was pleasantly "at home" here in the last frontier of Southwest Florida.

One

Who Was Barron Gift Collier?

The genius behind the creation of Collier County, Florida, from the untamed remote wilderness of the Everglades was indeed a visionary. Barron Gift Collier was born in Memphis, Tennessee, in 1873, the youngest son of Hannah and Cowles Collier. At 16, he left school and began the first of his many successful business ventures. Collier began with a street lighting business that would lead to printing and advertising in streetcars across the country through his Consolidated Street Railway Advertising Company in New York City. By age 26, Collier was a millionaire.

Collier married fellow Memphis-born socialite and longtime sweetheart Juliet Gordon Carnes on November 26, 1907, and they would have three sons: Barron Gift Jr., Samuel Carnes, and Cowles "Miles," who would later succeed him in his business ventures.

The Colliers first visited Lee County in 1911, and after a visit to Useppa Island, Collier purchased it from his friend John M. Roach. Collier was fascinated with Florida and its magical climate. He would also purchase the Deep Lake (grapefruit) grove and the railroad from Roach. Over the ensuing decade, from 1911 through 1921, Collier purchased more than one million acres of land, and upon his death in 1939, he was listed as the largest single landowner in Florida.

Collier's greatest accomplishment was the completion of the Tamiami Trail, connecting Tampa to Miami, which opened the area to both tourism and development on April 26, 1928. Collier also established the Southwest Mounted Police, who would patrol the wide, open completed road on Harley Davidson motorcycles, while assisting stranded motorists. He also built six way stations along the trail that served snacks and provided gasoline.

While the trail was under construction, Collier began developing his company town, called Everglades, which was incorporated as the original county seat in the newly established Collier County on May 8, 1923.

Collier rubbed shoulders with foreign dignitaries, former presidents, and other entrepreneurs, including Edison, Ford, Goodyear, and Wrigley (of chewing gum fame.)

A noticeably young Barron Gift Collier was born in Memphis, Tennessee, in 1873. Collier was named after two officers from his father's naval career, Commodore Samuel Barron and Lt. George Gift. As a young boy, Collier held a deep love of nature and roamed the Chickasaw Bluffs. (Courtesy of Lila Zuck.)

As a young man, Collier was questioned about why he left Memphis, and his reply was, "You cannot catch big fish in a bucket, meaning that you have to go where the big fish are." Beginning with street lamps and branching into streetcar advertising, Collier was soon on his way to becoming a millionaire by age 26. (Courtesy of Lila Zuck.)

Seen here is a more successful Barron Gift Collier, whose typical working day was 12 hours. He served as a special deputy police commissioner in New York City. But it was the primitive wilderness of Florida's last frontier that beckoned him. "What I want is wild country nobody wants. I can make it into a place where people will enjoy life," he was often quoted. (Courtesy of Collier County Museum.)

Following his first visit to Useppa Island, by invitation of John Roach, Barron Gift Collier bought the property for $100,000 in 1911. After discovering Roach had a grapefruit grove in the Everglades, he bought it as well. The area was known as Deep Lake, and this is the original canning label used at that time. (Courtesy of McKay Archives, Florida Southern College.)

Seen in this 1915 photograph is an unidentified participant in a parade from the small town of Deep Lake prior to Barron Gift Collier's ownership. Deep Lake was once a town located along the defunct Atlantic Coast Railroad at State Road 29 in Everglade, just north of today's Everglades City. The name came from the 95-foot-deep natural sinkhole dating back many years. (Courtesy of the State Archives of Florida.)

This original homestead belonged to pioneer William Smith Allen, and then George Storter Jr. purchased the property for $800 in 1889 and began taking in visiting sportsmen and fishermen, which resulted in the necessary additions for accommodations. This was the early beginnings of today's Rod & Gun Club, which was remodeled following Barron Gift Collier's ownership into a hunting and fishing lodge for his family and friends. (Courtesy of the State Archives of Florida.)

Barron Gift Collier promised the Florida State Legislature to complete the ongoing Tamiami Trail road project using his own personal funds in exchange for the creation of Collier County from a portion of southern Lee County. Collier County was established on May 8, 1923, and at the official signing, Collier was pictured standing, third from the left. (Courtesy of Collier County Museum.)

Two

Constructing Tamiami Trail with Blood, Sweat, and Mosquitoes

To look at the Tamiami Trail today, which runs from Tampa to Miami, one would not even pause to consider the actual blood, sweat, and tears from the more than 2,000 workers that went into the construction of this road that opened Southwest Florida to the masses. Barron Gift Collier began the last segment of the Tamiami Trail project in Collier County in 1923 and completed it at the Miami-Dade County line in 1928. Collier agreed to provide his own funding for the completion of the trail in exchange for the creation of Collier County from a portion of southern Lee County. Collier spared no expense in completing this project while providing the construction crews with the latest state-of-the-art equipment. And what they could not buy, his talented crew could make within their own headquarters located at Port DuPont, next to nearby Carnestown. Collier also made sure his work crews were served healthy meals, and he constructed not only a rolling mess hall for their meals, but also rolling bunkhouses to keep everyone on schedule.

After the initial surveying, the men worked in waist-deep muck and water, in the unrelenting heat under an unmerciful sun. An occasional rattlesnake or cottonmouth might startle one or more of the crew. Panthers and alligators were also a common and dangerous sight. These men fought off mosquitoes that swarmed in black clouds overhead day and night. But the worst of all these issues was the swamp rot on the workers' feet that resulted from standing in the water daily. They would be treated at the Juliet Carnes Collier Hospital, located on Storter Avenue in Everglades.

While work was underway on the trail, Collier began work on six way stations located along the trail at 10-to-12-mile intervals and hired six husband-and-wife crews to assist these early travelers along the wide-open trail.

The work began in October 1923, and the finished road opened at a cost of $8 million, with a celebratory parade held on April 26, 1928, in Everglades.

The arduous task of constructing the Tamiami Trail fell first to the surveyors. Once they were finished, the crews began by cutting the impenetrable scrub brush with machetes. Stakes were driven into the ground approximately 100 feet apart to mark the center of the road. The clearing crews came next. (Courtesy of Naples Historical Society, Inc.)

All the trees in the path of the road had to be cut down using two-man saws and dragged clear of the right-of-way by oxen teams, as seen above. Throughout the five-year project, begun in 1923, a team of 40 oxen was always on hand. The dynamite used on the building of the Tamiami Trail was 50 percent of the construction cost. Nearly three million sticks of dynamite were used on this project, one entire freight car load every three weeks. If the muck was impassable for the oxen, the workers laid down wooden rails, as seen below, and they would push the car loaded with the dynamite. (Above, courtesy of Collier County Museum; below, courtesy of the State Archives of Florida.)

Steam shovels were also used in the construction of the Tamiami Trail. Barron Gift Collier had two warehouses constructed, one in Carnestown and the other in Port DuPont, stocked with spare parts for the various machines building the trail. (Courtesy of the State Archives of Florida.)

Another piece of equipment used in the construction of the Tamiami Trail was this drill rig. For 28 months, there would be three drill rigs and two compressors running 24 hours a day. (Courtesy of the State Archives of Florida.)

Port DuPont was the "nerve center" during the construction of the Tamiami Trail. This warehouse at Port DuPont was stocked with spare parts for the machines building the trail. Blacksmiths worked constantly to rebuild what the Everglades destroyed. It had been repeatedly stated that without the port facilities and numerous shops on hand, it would have been impossible to build the trail. This image was taken in 1926. (Courtesy of Collier County Museum.)

A driller work crew, above, pauses briefly for a group photograph; unfortunately, no names were included. A special machine was created to drill dynamite holes into the solid rock base. This machine was mounted on rails that were taken up and relaid as it advanced. The drilling machine constantly ran, day and night, for 28 months, averaging about 250 feet per day. The sign below, posted along the Tamiami Trail, brought smiles to many faces. Each day of construction brought its own new numbers, trying to surpass the previous days' work. But the message and mantra were clear: "On to Miami!" Common laborers received 20¢ per hour, and drivers received 25¢ per hour. The photographs were taken from 1923 to 1928 during the road construction period. (Both, courtesy of Naples Historical Society, Inc.)

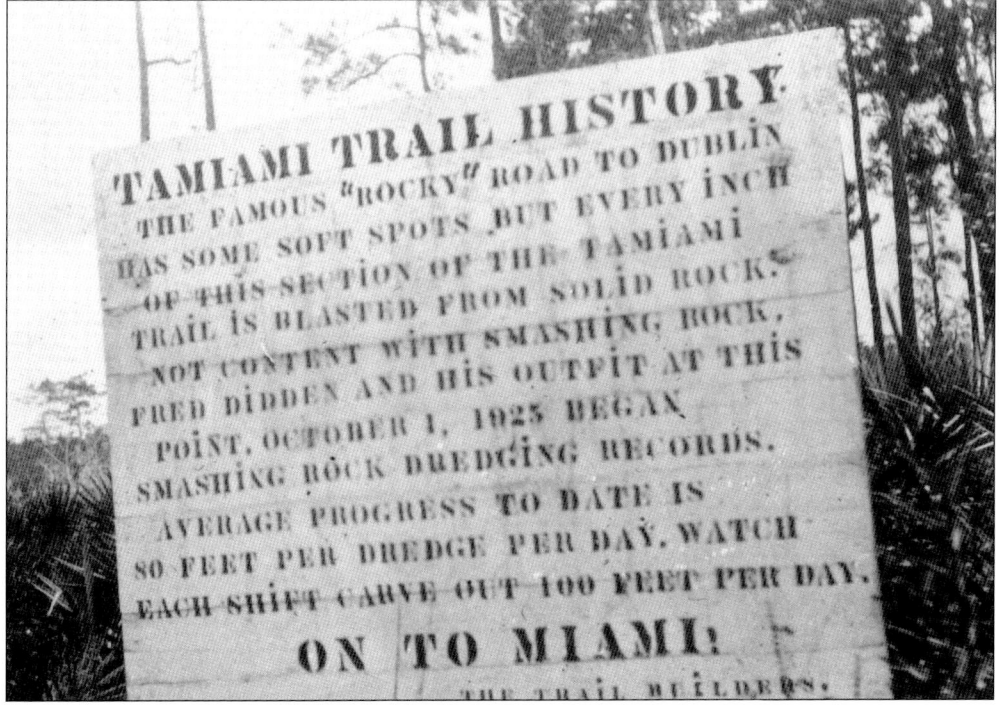

The harder the rock, the more sticks of dynamite were used. Nearly three million sticks of dynamite were used on this Tamiami Trail construction project—one entire freight car load every three weeks. It was said if the dynamite sticks were placed end to end, it would have reached from Tampa, Florida, to San Francisco, California. (Courtesy of Collier County Museum.)

This Bay City walking dredge, made in Bay City, Michigan, was used on the construction of the Tamiami Trail and named a National Historic Mechanical Engineering Landmark. Visitors to the Collier-Seminole State Park can view the Bay City walking dredge up close and personal. (Courtesy of the State Archives of Florida.)

Collier bought three of the Bay City walking dredges, and these were used in tandem to speed up the work along the Tamiami Trail. The one-cubic-yard buckets each dredge had maintained an average useful life of two weeks. These dredges worked two 10-hour shifts per day. The two-hour down period was scheduled between shifts in order to inspect, service, and repair these machines. (Courtesy of the State Archives of Florida.)

It seems Barron Gift Collier thought of everything, especially when it came to his Tamiami Trail road crews. Laborers working far from town were provided with portable bunkhouses and home cooking. Wild turkeys and venison were occasionally purchased from the local Indians as supplements. Fresh food and ice were brought in daily from Port DuPont. (Courtesy of Collier County Museum.)

This is an interior shot of the mobile mess hall used during the construction of the Tamiami Trail. Three mess hall dining cars provided meals around the clock. (Courtesy of Naples Historical Society, Inc.)

Rolling Bunkhouses—Work crew bunkhouses were pulled forward by oxen on the rough right-of-way an average of 150 feet a day. These were the first mobile homes in a state now numbering them in millions (courtesy of Collier Development Corporation).

These work crew bunkhouses were pulled forward by oxen on the rough right-of-way along the Tamiami Trail at an average of 150 feet per day. They were considered the first mobile homes in a state now numbering them in the millions. (Courtesy of Collier County Museum.)

The two way stations pictured here, Weaver's Camp (above) and Royal Palm Hammock (below), along with four others, were built in the late 1920s to assist those travelers driving through the remote regions of Collier County along the Tamiami Trail. Keep in mind there were no houses or businesses along this stretch of road back then, and the very rough gravel roads were wide open and not heavily trafficked yet. Many a wild animal—including bears, panthers, and alligators—could pose problems to drivers unaccustomed to this wilderness, especially out on the open road. Gasoline, snacks, and other conveniences were available to drivers. Following the Great Depression, Collier disbanded the Southwest Mounted Police and sold the way stations. (Both. courtesy of Big Cypress National Preserve.)

30

The Monroe Station (above) operated until 1949 and then closed in the 1980s amid environmental concerns over the gasoline tanks on the property now owned by the National Park Service. The station was added to the National Register of Historical Places in 2000. The station had been boarded up for many years. On April 9, 2016, at approximately 11:45 p.m., firefighters and law enforcement personnel responded to a fire at Monroe Station. Three men from Miami had come to the station to take photographs. One of the men climbed up on the roof and began "spinning," and in no time, this historic way station was gone. The Paolita Station, shown below in a photograph postcard, stood along the Tamiami Trail near the Miami-Dade County line. (Above, courtesy of Lila Zuck; below, courtesy of Robert S. Carr.)

This unidentified Southwest Mounted Policeman poses for the camera in 1933 on his county-issued Harley Davidson motorcycle in his colorful uniform of a scarlet tunic, black pants, and a county Mountie-style hat modeled after the Canadian Mounted Police. One policeman was positioned at each of the way stations along the Tamiami Trail, where he patrolled a 10-mile stretch on his motorcycle. (Courtesy of the State Archives of Florida.)

THE SOUTHWEST MOUNTED
(Fort Myers Tropical News.)

The problems of traffic and public safety which arise with the opening of the Tamiami Trail through the wilderness of Collier county are to be met with measures quite in keeping with the magnitude of that colossal highway project. A patrol of motorcycle officers will be organized to control traffic on what is probably the greatest uninterrupted stretch of standard highway in the world, to protect travelers from the possibility of marauders and to make impossible the stranding of motorists in the depths of the Everglades. Filling stations at appropriate intervals will take the place for the time being of the towns and villages to which motorists are accustomed.

Only those who have made the trip over the new road from Naples to Miami, a distance of more than 100 miles, can appreciate the importance of an adequate patrol system. Except for Carnestown, which is only a construction camp, there is no settlement in this entire district. Everglades, the county seat of Collier county, is three miles south of Carnestown and the trail. The temptation to extravagant speed will naturally be great since the turns are few and gentle, but a menace to the reckless lurks in the drainage canal along the trail. The canal in places is almost 20 feet deep. We need have no particular fear of marauders and bandits in this day and age, but the presence of an alert motor patrol will be reassuring. The "Southwest Mounted Police" will have its hands full when the trail is opened and becomes, as we hope, one of the most heavily traveled highways in the country.

Pictured here is an April 13, 1926, newspaper article on the Southwest Mounted Police, whose territory ran along the Tamiami Trail. (Courtesy of the State Archives of Florida.)

Above, the townspeople and guests are here and ready to celebrate the completion and grand opening of the incredulous Tamiami Trail project following five long years of work. The two-story building in the center is the town jail, and the structure at the far end of the street is the Atlantic Coast Line Railroad Depot. Below, the lady and her horse are gearing up for their placement in the parade. The building behind her is the Bank of Everglades. The official celebration was held, complete with a band and grand parade, on April 26, 1928. (Both, courtesy of the State Archives of Florida.)

Celebrating the completion of the Tamiami Trail on April 26, 1928, Barron Gift Collier and Florida governor John W. Martin lead this roughly 500-car convoy heading south toward the Miami-Dade County line. Various notable dignitaries with ties to Florida were on hand, including Henry Ford, Thomas Edison, John Ringling, and others, were responsible for the opening celebrations." (Courtesy of HistoryMiami Museum.)

The stone archway above consists of lime rock that was blasted to make way for the Tamiami Trail construction. It served as the dividing line between Collier County and Miami-Dade County. It appears to have been constructed around the completion of the trail in 1928. The lengthy convoy drove through the archway over to Miami to continue the celebration of the completion of the Tamiami Trail on April 26, 1928. Numerous cars that lined up following the parade can be seen below. (Both, courtesy of the State Archives of Florida.)

One lone motorist crosses the Tamiami Trail. The note on the back of the photograph, taken on March 24, 1930, states, "An almost perfectly level road for over 100 miles, with a canal running alongside, crosses the Everglades connecting Tampa and Miami." The canals were built for drainage, irrigation, and flood control. The Tamiami Trail remains a two-lane road. (Courtesy of the State Archives of Florida.)

This commemorative postal envelope from 1988 highlights the 60th anniversary of the completion of the Tamiami Trail in 1928. It is interesting to note that in addition to showcasing Barron Gift Collier, founder and financier, an illustration of the historic walking dredge is depicted, along with a listing of the way stations that dispensed gasoline and snacks to travelers along the trail. (Courtesy of Collier County Museum.)

TAMIAMI TRAIL

THE TAMIAMI TRAIL LINKS THE TWO GREAT CITIES FOR WHICH IT WAS NAMED--TAMPA AND MIAMI. IT BRIDGES THE EVERGLADES, TYING TOGETHER SOUTH FLORIDA'S ATLANTIC AND GULF COASTS.

ITS OFFICIAL OPENING ON APRIL 25, 1928, BY GOVERNOR JOHN W. MARTIN CLIMAXED THIRTEEN YEARS OF PLANNING AND WORKING.

FLORIDA IS INDEBTED TO CAPTAIN J. F. JAUDON, WHOSE FAITH AND PERSISTENCE KEPT THE PROJECT ALIVE; TO THE INTREPID TRAIL BLAZERS, WHOSE TRIP BY CAR ACROSS THE TRACKLESS EVERGLADES IN 1923 DRAMATIZED THE NEED FOR THE HIGHWAY'S COMPLETION; TO BARRON G. COLLIER FOR HIS UNSTINTING AID, AND TO OTHERS WHOSE TIME, ENERGIES AND TALENTS MADE THIS TREMENDOUS FEAT POSSIBLE.

THE HISTORICAL ASSOCIATION OF SOUTHERN FLORIDA--1958

This bronze marker, provided by the Historical Association of Southern Florida in 1958, can be viewed along the Tamiami Trail in Carnestown, just past the traffic light at the intersection of the trail and State Road 29. The official opening of the Tamiami Trail was held on April 26, 1928. (Courtesy of the State Archives of Florida.)

134 THE TAMIAMI TRAIL, FLORIDA.

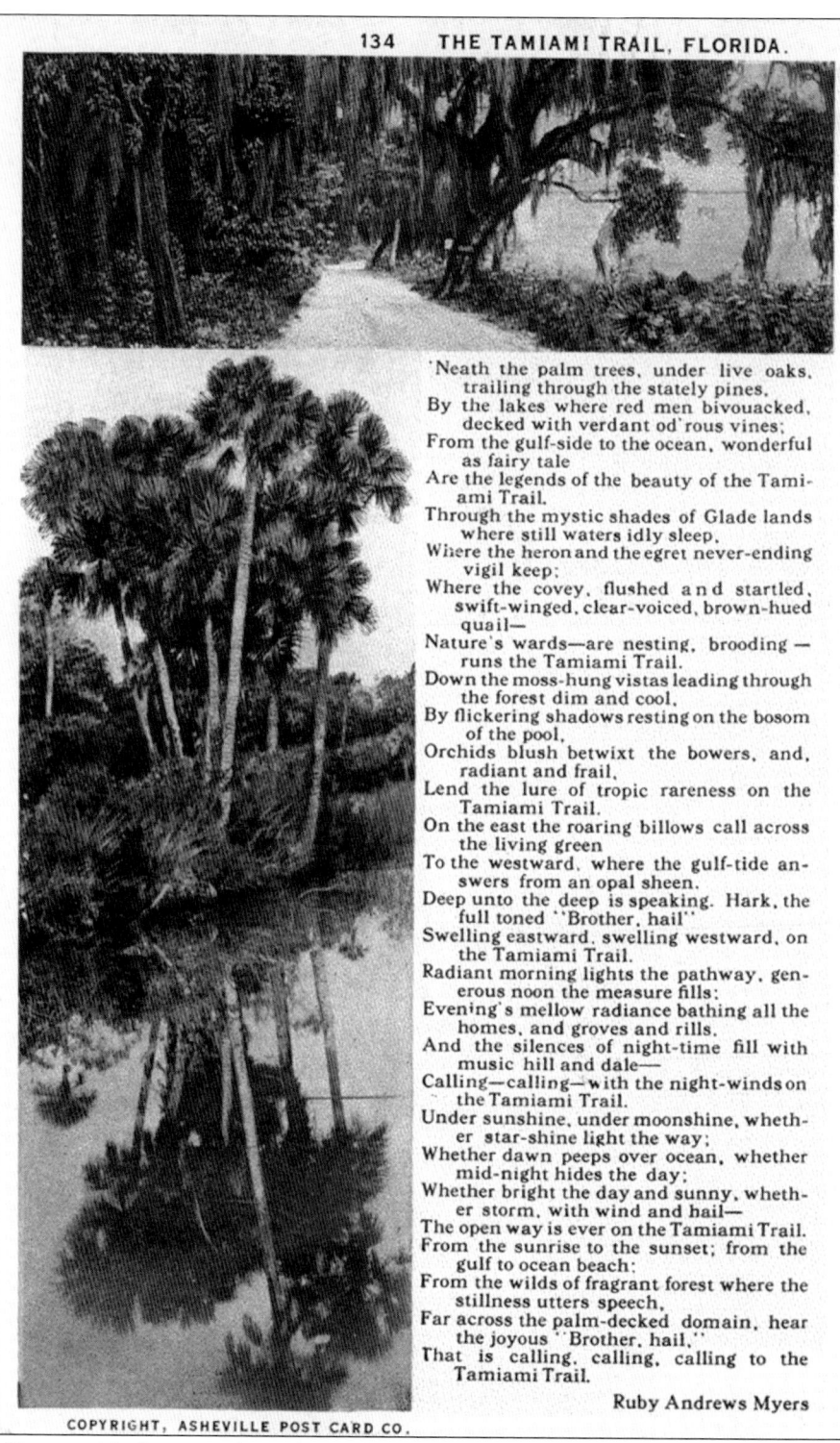

'Neath the palm trees, under live oaks,
  trailing through the stately pines,
By the lakes where red men bivouacked,
  decked with verdant od'rous vines;
From the gulf-side to the ocean, wonderful
  as fairy tale
Are the legends of the beauty of the Tamiami Trail.
Through the mystic shades of Glade lands
  where still waters idly sleep,
Where the heron and the egret never-ending
  vigil keep;
Where the covey, flushed and startled,
  swift-winged, clear-voiced, brown-hued
  quail—
Nature's wards—are nesting, brooding —
  runs the Tamiami Trail.
Down the moss-hung vistas leading through
  the forest dim and cool,
By flickering shadows resting on the bosom
  of the pool,
Orchids blush betwixt the bowers, and,
  radiant and frail,
Lend the lure of tropic rareness on the
  Tamiami Trail.
On the east the roaring billows call across
  the living green
To the westward, where the gulf-tide an-
  swers from an opal sheen,
Deep unto the deep is speaking. Hark, the
  full toned "Brother, hail"
Swelling eastward, swelling westward, on
  the Tamiami Trail.
Radiant morning lights the pathway, gen-
  erous noon the measure fills;
Evening's mellow radiance bathing all the
  homes, and groves and rills,
And the silences of night-time fill with
  music hill and dale—
Calling—calling—with the night-winds on
  the Tamiami Trail.
Under sunshine, under moonshine, wheth-
  er star-shine light the way;
Whether dawn peeps over ocean, whether
  mid-night hides the day;
Whether bright the day and sunny, wheth-
  er storm, with wind and hail—
The open way is ever on the Tamiami Trail.
From the sunrise to the sunset; from the
  gulf to ocean beach;
From the wilds of fragrant forest where the
  stillness utters speech,
Far across the palm-decked domain, hear
  the joyous "Brother, hail,"
That is calling, calling, calling to the
  Tamiami Trail.

Ruby Andrews Myers

COPYRIGHT, ASHEVILLE POST CARD CO.

This Tamiami Trail poem is by Ruby Andrews Myers and is found on this postcard from 1923. (Courtesy of the State Archives of Florida.)

TAMIAMI TRAIL

Have you been noticing the great activity along the Tamiami Trail? That great, new Cross State Highway. Do you realize what the widening to 70 feet through Miami and the surfacing into a fine, smooth Boulevard clear across to the West Coast will mean?

Do you know that Dade County has telegraphed for machinery to finish our portion of the Trail—that over 300 miles are finished on the other end—that the Chevelier Corporation is working day and night with huge road-making outfits to finish their part and Collier County is doing likewise?

With traffic twice as heavy as now uses the Dixie Highway passing along the Trail, where will the price of bordering land go to? How long will you be able to buy at today's prices? Tomorrow! Perhaps—and perhaps not. WAIT—and pay the fellow who buys now a nice fat profit.

Wake up—act and buy Tamiami Trail frontage—buy NOW—prices along the Trail are not going down.

I have 140 acres fronting on the Trail and Canal, which I would like to buy myself, but as I cannot handle it, I am offering it for quick sale at only $68.00 per acre. Total $9,520 on terms of only $1,500 cash, $1,000 in six months, $2,340 in one year, $2,340 in 2 years and $2,340 in 3 years.

This tract should double in value long before it is paid for.

If you want this—better bring your check book.

For sale exclusively by

Henry H. Sprague, Realtor

216 N. E. 2nd Ave.　　　　　　　　　　Phone 4380.

This Tamiami Trail realtor advertisement was posted in the newspapers. (Courtesy of the State Archives of Florida.)

Barron Gift Collier was so grateful to the Seminole Indians, shown above, for their assistance during the construction of the Tamiami Trail that he provided them with free fares on his Trailways Bus Line. (Courtesy of Naples Historical Society, Inc.)

Three

CREATING THE COMPANY TOWN OF EVERGLADES

It was most important to county namesake Barron Gift Collier that his company town of Everglades had a bank for both local businesses and families. Equally important was a hospital to help those with injuries sustained from working on the Tamiami Trail road construction or in the local fields or from any other accidents. A laundry was essential, too, to clean not only the town workers' uniforms, but also the restaurant linens from both the Everglades Inn and the Rod & Gun Club. Naturally, a government courthouse was a necessity. The town also required a grocery, movie theater, and a nondenominational church to round it out. The Atlantic Coast Line Railroad Depot operated for 30-plus years following its opening in 1928. Although Collier's initial plans were grandiose, envisioning a town of approximately 5,000 people, not only did he not live to see his plans come to fruition, but the town has maintained its approximate 500 residential annual population for numerous decades.

With the Tamiami Trail road construction progressing, Collier needed someone who could manage all of his projects, big and small, and he found this talent in US Naval Academy graduate David Graham Copeland. He was a brilliant civil engineer who rose to Collier's challenge and transformed this area within a few short years, adding a school, newspaper, retail shops, electricity, and regular mail service while also keeping the trail construction on schedule.

Interestingly, both the bank (1974) and the laundry (2001) are listed in the National Register of Historic Places.

Collier brought a touch of class into the area with the Everglades Inn and its dry goods shops, dining restaurant, café, drugstore, hardware, and sundries, the likes that had never been seen before nor likely will again. Collier discovered maître d' Claus "Snooky" Senghaas while in Germany and managed to lure him to tiny Everglades to manage both restaurants. Snooky was all about the experience of either dining or fishing, and a journal filled with grateful guests' notes could attest to his attentiveness to even the smallest detail.

Seen here is an early c. 1950 aerial of Everglades City, Florida, and the Ten Thousand Islands. In the upper left-hand corner, the arrow indicates nearby Chokoloskee Island, Florida. The causeway to connect the two communities was not completed until 1956. (Courtesy of Collier County Museum.)

Young, dashing US Naval Academy graduate David Graham Copeland (left) is pictured upon his arrival to the Everglades in the 1920s. Otto Neal, beside him with the white hat, was an engineer for Barron Gift Collier. Copeland took the challenge to manage all of Collier's projects, including both the Tamiami Trail and the company town of Everglades. (Courtesy of Lila Zuck.)

Above is an early photograph of the original Collier County Courthouse, built in 1928. It remained in use until 1962, when the government seat was moved to nearby Naples. Afterward, it was renamed Everglades City Hall (below) and maintains that name today. Additionally, the council chambers, both the mayor's and city clerk's offices, along with the building official office and the planning and zoning office, are located here. There is also a library branch in addition to the Betterment Association and the Everglades Society for Historical Preservation offices. The Everglades City Hall photograph was taken in 2007 following repairs and improvements after Hurricane Wilma's destructive hit in 2005. (Above, courtesy of the State Archives of Florida; below, photograph by author.)

The Bank of Everglades, located on West Broadway, opened for business on July 7, 1923, as a member of the FDIC (Federal Deposit Insurance Corporation). It was the only bank in Collier County until 1949. It remained the sole bank in Everglades City until 1962, following the sale of the bank's charter and subsequent move to Immokalee. The only remaining item left behind in Everglades City is the original 3,000-pound safe (right). In the ensuing years, the building has been home to several bed-and-breakfasts, and at one time, a person could rent out a room there. It is empty at this writing. The Bank of Everglades was listed in the National Register of Historic Places in 1974. (Above, courtesy of the State Archives of Florida; right, photograph by author.)

The Everglades Model Steam Laundry opened in October 1927 and was the featured story on the front page of the *Collier County News* touting its state-of-the-art equipment. In addition to offering both wet and dry cleaning, the workers also provided custom tailoring and alterations. The laundry was operated by the Echols and Ayres families until it closed during World War II for lack of supplies and help. Above is an exterior shot of the laundry with various unidentified workers. The unidentified newspaper reporter shared that all water used in these special machines is coming from a local well and, therefore, does not require any softeners or chemicals. In the below interior shot of the laundry, various bins are in use. (Both, courtesy of Collier County Museum.)

The Model Steam Laundry & Dry Cleaning truck, used for deliveries in and around Everglades, is seen above. Family member Ron Echols of Naples identified the following workers in this c. 1930s image. From left to right are Virgil Smith, Janelle "Judy" Echols, unidentified girl, Leroy Echols, Frances Echols, Annie Merle Echols, and Myrtle Deloach Echols (an aunt to the Echols). After the laundry shuttered its doors, the building was leased to an insurance company until Hurricane Donna hit in 1960, sending six feet of water everywhere. By 1965, the local Everglades Women's Club began meeting there and later decided to purchase the building in 1972. Pictured below is the exterior of the structure when it was home to the club. (Above, courtesy of Collier County Museum; below, courtesy of the State Archives of Florida.)

After disbanding in 1988, several members of the Everglades Women's Club decided to deed the building to the county and turn it into a local museum. These same women spent the next decade holding various fundraisers to bring this museum to fruition. The sign posted in front of the renovated building states the museum is coming soon. This photograph was taken in 1994. (Photograph by author.)

A decade later, the Museum of the Everglades opened on April 26, 1998. In September 2001, the museum was added to the National Register of Historic Places. It also became the first satellite museum in Collier County. (Photograph by author.)

The original Everglades Depot (above), opened in 1928, was just one more important component of Barron Gift Collier's successful company town. The second floor held the living quarters for the stationmaster. Carrying both freight and passengers, the trains enabled the local farmers to ship their goods both quicker and at much farther distances. The train not only moved people and freight, it also delivered the mail. It was operational until 1956. The Atlantic Coast Line Railroad station (below) was the terminus of Broadway, looking due east, shown with a freight train pulling into the station. (Above, courtesy of the State Archives of Florida; below, courtesy of Collier County Museum.)

Florida author Gregg M. Turner shared in his book Images of America: *Railroads of Southwest Florida* that a "combination baggage-coach car ran from Everglades, dubbed the southernmost point on the Coast Line system, to Immokalee. Thirty-two people could be accommodated, but it lacked air conditioning." After the Atlantic Coast Line Railroad closed, the depot fell into private hands. This photograph was taken around 1944. (Courtesy of Collier County Museum.)

The Everglades Community Church, known as "the friendly little church on the circle," has been a nondenominational church since 1939, when the land was offered by the Collier Corporation to the community with the stipulation that a church be built by 1940 and that it remain nondenominational. This image was captured in May 1957. (Courtesy of the State Archives of Florida.)

The Juliet Carnes Collier Hospital officially opened in 1923, the same year Collier County was created, and was named after Barron Gift Collier's wife. It was equipped with the latest in modern medical equipment. After suffering through the 1926 hurricane, a new location was found for the hospital. During the hospital's 40 years of service, it weathered two devastating hurricanes and the Great Depression. (Courtesy of Collier County Museum.)

Seen in the above c. 1948 photograph is the former Everglades Inn & Manhattan Mercantile storefront on the ground floor in Everglades City, located on the corners of West Broadway and Allen Avenue. Dubbed Barron Gift Collier's "business district," it was built in 1924. The view below shows both the restaurant and café side entrances. The ground floor housed the Mercantile department store, a drugstore and pharmacy, Win-Car (hardware), and a sundries shop. In less than an hour, the historic building was gone following an early morning fire on May 11, 1987. Win-Car was the only business that survived, and it relocated to Collier Avenue. (Above, courtesy Collier County Museum; below, courtesy of State Archives of Florida.)

Seen above is the interior of the Manhattan Mercantile Corporation Drugstore, located on the ground floor of the Everglades Inn on West Broadway in Everglades City. The pharmacy is located on the left, with the marble-top counter and soda fountain on the right. Below is an interior shot of the Manhattan Mercantile Corporation Dry Goods Store with two unidentified salesclerks among the shelves and display cases filled with assorted merchandise. (Both, courtesy of Collier County Museum.)

The interior of the Everglades Inn dining room in Everglades City is seen above. This inn, managed by Chef "Snooky" Senghaas, was touted as the "social hub" and the place where everyone wanted to be seen. Snooky was the consummate planner and loved creating surprises for his guests. The tables are set ready for guests, and both chandeliers and electric fans were in use. Note that under the serving table on the right is a Flit, a brand-name insecticide gun that was used to control mosquitoes between 1928 and the mid-1950s. Exterior shot of the former Everglades Inn's Sundries shop is shown at left. The upper two floors offered both apartments and rentals. (Above, courtesy of Naples Historical Society, Inc.; left, courtesy of the State Archives of Florida.)

Everglades City's historic Rod & Gun Club had humble beginnings in 1864. Upon Barron Gift Collier's purchase of the Storter property in the early 1920s, it was renamed and redesigned as a private fine dining establishment for Collier's family and friends. Upon entering the building today, visitors can see the walls literally papered with newspaper articles about the club's history over the years. (Courtesy of the State Archives of Florida.)

In 1923, while vacationing in Germany, Barron Gift Collier caught the eye of young maître d' Snooky Senghaas and successfully lured him to come work for him in Everglades. In addition to working at the Everglades Inn, Snooky also worked at the renovated Rod & Gun Club. Soon after his arrival, he was creating some of the best talked-about meals in the area, preparing dishes that included pompano, trout, wild turkey, and venison, all of which were in plentiful supply then. Snooky became quite the legendary figure while at the helm of the Rod & Gun Club until his premature death in 1954 at the young age of 57. His legendary meals fed former presidents Herbert H. Hoover, Harry S. Truman, and Dwight D. Eisenhower. Snooky is seen at left on the docks at the Rod & Gun Club. The image below shows the master host at the bar inside the Rod & Gun Club. (Both, courtesy of Collier County Museum.)

Upon discovering a journal (seen below) that Snooky kept for guests at the Rod & Gun Club to sign, along with any comments relative to their lodging or fishing trips, one signature in particular stood out, stating "It's very exciting to catch your first tarpon after years of trolling (or however you spell it) but it's about as satisfying to discover that Mrs. Senghaas provides the finest coffee in the known world. There really isn't any coffee like it," signed Marjory Stoneman Douglas on July 5, 1936. The same Marjory Stoneman Douglas of Miami, Florida (right), environmentalist, philanthropist, and author of the bestselling *The Everglades: River of Grass* that first opened the reader's eyes to the importance of the Everglades and the need to protect it. Her book was published in 1947. (Right, courtesy of the State Archives of Florida; below, courtesy of Collier County Museum.)

This photograph shows riders boarding the Everglades streetcar that was in service in 1928. The town of Everglades had the distinction of operating the only streetcar on the west coast of Florida, south of Tampa. The battery-powered car ran between Everglades and Port DuPont, near the Tamiami Trail. Former local schoolchildren often rode the streetcar to and from their school, which taught kindergarten through 12th grade. (Courtesy of Collier County Museum.)

Four

PLUME HUNTING, MOONSHINE, AND SQUARE GROUPER

Collier County has seen seven sheriffs since its incorporation, and four served while Everglades was still the county seat. The original four sheriffs included Capt. W.R. Maynard (1923–1928), Lewis J. Thorp (1928–1954), Roy O. Atkins (1954–1956), and E.A. "Doug" Hendry (1956–1975). Each brought his own style and sense of duty to the role. Throughout these 60-plus years, it was their job, as sheriff, to maintain and keep the peace through often trying times, from plume-hunting days and running moonshine to rum-running and the Operation Everglades drug bust in the early 1980s. These illegal activities were coupled with the normal vagrancy, speeding tickets, domestic arrests, petty theft, and other charges in a town with roughly 500 residents.

Under Maynard's reign, Collier was in its infancy and dubbed "Florida's Last Frontier." While Barron Gift Collier was constructing the Tamiami Trail, he also built six way stations, today's equivalent of a rest stop, along the trail for aid to those in need. These six men who lived at the way stations began as the Southwest Mounted Police and were later deputized as county deputies. After Maynard resigned, Thorp was appointed and learned he could keep the frontier feel with his expertise of a bullwhip until his death. Atkins would also be appointed but served only one term and died after a short illness. Hendry would become the longest-serving sheriff, running until his ill health forced his resignation.

Before the county seat was relocated to nearby Naples in 1962, Everglades had seen two local jails in operation.

Barron Gift Collier handpicked William Riley "W.R." Maynard as his first sheriff in 1923. There were no paved roads or electricity in "Florida's Last Frontier." A veteran of World War I, with a pilot's license, Maynard was called the "flying sheriff." Maynard arrested 10 people in his first three months on the job, without even a jail. (Courtesy of Capt. Thomas B. Smith, Collier County Sheriff's Alumni Association.)

Gov. John W. Martin appointed Lewis J. Thorp, seen at right, as the second Collier County sheriff in 1928. Thorp was sheriff during Prohibition days, which had begun in the early 1920s and led to an increase in the illegal production and sale of liquor, often known as bootlegging. Hunting these bootleggers kept the sheriff's office quite busy. He served until his death in 1953 while still in office, making him the longest-tenured sheriff in the county's history. Following Thorp's death, Roy O. Atkins, pictured below, was appointed sheriff until a special election was held. Atkins's tenure was short. Prior to becoming the sheriff, Atkins came to Florida in 1923 to work with the US Army Corps of Engineers on Lake Okeechobee. Both sheriffs were primarily peacekeepers, enforcing liquor laws and maintaining order. (Right, courtesy of Capt. Thomas B. Smith, Collier County Sheriff's Alumni Association; below, courtesy of Lila Zuck.)

E.A. "Doug" Hendry was elected Collier County's fourth sheriff in 1956. Hendry was a war hero who had received five Bronze Stars and a Purple Heart from his European tour in 1943–1945 while serving under Gen. George S. Patton. He returned to his hometown of Fort Myers, Florida, following the war and a decade later became the new sheriff of Collier County, with a population of 12,000 and its county seat located in Everglades City. He would continue to hold office for the next 19 years, resigning in 1975 due to ill health. (Courtesy of Capt. Thomas B. Smith, Collier County Sheriff's Alumni Association.)

The two-story building above, seen from the Collier County Courthouse across the town's circle, was the original Collier County jail, photographed in 1932 with Deputy Bill Hutto standing in front. It was built in 1928 and faithfully served this community until it was replaced with a more modern jail in 1951; the new jail was located next door to the former courthouse, now known as Everglades City Hall. The second jail, shown in the 1994 aerial shot below, can be seen at the bottom left-hand side, the L-shaped building next to city hall. (Above, courtesy of Lila Zuck; below, photograph by author.)

By 1886, the numbers showed that birds were being killed at a rate of five million per year—for women's hats. Guy Bradley (left) had moved to Florida and was recommended for the position of game warden for Monroe County and hired. Just three short years into his job, Bradley heard gunshots nearby on July 8, 1905, and set out to investigate. He would once again encounter a father, Walter Smith, and his two sons shooting up the rookery. The father shot and killed Bradley. Bradley's senseless death, along with two other game wardens, helped encourage the passage of the Audubon Plumage Act of 1910, outlawing the plume trade. The biggest "prized" bird was the snowy egret (below). (Left, courtesy of the State Archives of Florida; below, courtesy of Rookery Bay Estuarine Research Reserve.)

Several cameramen on location in Everglades City, Florida, film *Wind Across the Everglades*. Screenwriter Budd Schulberg, whose credits include *On the Waterfront*, is shown in the left foreground. The film debuted in Miami, Florida, in August 1958. Rumor has it that the local chickens were given extra feathers in order to portray the egrets. (Courtesy of the State Archives of Florida.)

Pictured above are, from left to right actor Burl Ives, local Florida hermit Roy Ozmer, and actor Tony Galento on location in Pelican Key, Florida, during filming of *Wind Across the Everglades.* The film was loosely based on the real life of Audubon game warden Guy Bradley, who was killed in the line of duty in 1905 for protecting Florida's plumed birds. Filming began in 1957, and for three months, the residents were given a glimpse into the world of celebrity. Every room at the Rod & Gun Club was rented during the filming. Screenwriter Budd Schulberg, in the photograph at left, speaks with actor Christopher Plummer (right) on location during the filming of *Wind Across the Everglades.* Historical records show that bird plumes sold for $32 an ounce in 1915, the same rate as gold. (Both, courtesy of the State Archives of Florida.)

Even before Collier County was incorporated in 1923, moonshine was very prevalent in the Everglades due to its remoteness, beginning with Prohibition in the 1920s and continuing up to the mid-1950s. In the above c. early 1930s photograph, Sheriff Lewis Thorp is on the right, accompanied by another deputy, showcasing the haul of moonshine they had just confiscated in Everglades. In Chokoloskee-native Totch Brown's book, *Totch: A Life in the Everglades*, he freely talks about his own father's stills and staying one step above the law. In the photograph below are Deputy Sheriff Roy Atkins accompanied by his wife, Helen, following yet another moonshine raid in 1934. The truck used for transporting the confiscated haul belonged to the Everglades Laundry. (Above, courtesy of the State Archives of Florida; below, courtesy of Lila Zuck.)

In the early morning hours of July 7, 1983, more than 200 federal and state agents, including the Collier County Sheriff's Office (CCSO), Drug Enforcement Administration (DEA), US Coast Guard (USCG), Federal Bureau of Investigation (FBI), Florida's National Guard, and the Internal Revenue Service (IRS), swept across Everglades City in one of the nation's biggest marijuana smuggling crackdowns, dubbed Operation Everglades, netting 28 smugglers. Agents also seized 3 small airplanes and 15 boats, along with an assortment of cars and trucks used in the transportation of marijuana smuggling. The local mosquito-infested mangrove islands proved to be the ideal place for reeling in "square grouper," a local term describing the compressed bales of marijuana (above). Local law enforcement agents are seen below hauling the marijuana before locking it up. (Above, author's collection; below, courtesy of Capt. Thomas B. Smith, Collier County Sheriff's Alumni Association.)

This 1953 photograph of the Everglades Airpark shows a simple landing strip. It would stay much the same for another 50 years. Due to its remoteness, one can see how easy it would be for marijuana smugglers to move their drugs from this landing strip and how three small airplanes could be seized by federal agents during Operation Everglades on July 7, 1983. (Courtesy of the State Archives of Florida.)

Welcome to the Everglades Airport! That is what the sign reads in the above photograph, taken in 1994. One can see the makeshift terminal beyond the sign posted at the entrance to the former landing strip. In the aerial photograph below, also taken in 1994, one can see the landing strip's extension from previous days as well as additional community growth. On November 18, 1996, a community-wide grand opening ceremony was held to celebrate its $1 million face-lift, which transformed it into an official airpark. The face-lift included the construction of a 1,000-square-foot terminal, security fence and gate, water and sewer lines, an automated self-fuel farm, aircraft storage facility, taxiway and helipad, and airplane parking on the 30-acre parcel of land. (Both, photograph by author.)

Five

INSPIRING PIONEER WOMEN OF THE EVERGLADES

Women have always played a large part in Collier County's history and have many incredible stories to share. These were women of strength and fortitude. Women who made a difference. Women who made their surroundings a better place for everyone.

At the age of 57, Deaconess Harriet Bedell was invited to Miami, Florida, from her then-current residence in Alaska to speak on behalf of the Alaskan Chain of Missions. Bedell found her calling after touring a Seminole reservation in Everglades and would spend her remaining days focusing on the living conditions of the Miccosukee and Seminole Indians.

Clara McKay, affectionately known locally as "Mama Hokie," arrived in Ochopee, Florida, from Miami, Florida, to help her husband, Sam, open a trailer camp business along Tamiami Trail. Hokie faced death twice alone and lived to tell her stories.

As the daughter of a fisherman, young Jimmie House Robinson knew the hard life and trials of a fisherman, yet she married one. She organized a group of local fishermen before expanding throughout the state of Florida while creating the Organized Fishermen of Florida (OFF). Implementing proper laws to protect both the fisherman and the fishing industry was their goal. Robinson lobbied in Tallahassee, Florida, often taking her two young children with her, in a borrowed car.

Elva McGill was one-half of the Tamiami Trail way station operators who manned the Paolita Station, offering light refreshment as well as pumping gasoline to travelers in need while living above the station, situated next to the Miami-Dade County line. Almost daily, she would go out the back door with rifle in hand and shoot their supper. McGill was loved and respected by everyone.

As Collier County's first female law enforcement officer, Blanche Maynard's mettle was tested after three convicts escaped the county jail and fled in 1923. Strapping on her sidearm, she quickly organized a posse and set off in hot pursuit—with her two-year-old son in tow. She recaptured and marched them back to jail and locked them up.

Deaconess Harriet Bedell stands in front of the door to the Glade Cross Mission in Everglades City, Florida, in April 1958. It was here in this mission that Bedell taught and healed the Miccosukee and Seminole Indians as well as led them to Christianity. She would remain here until Hurricane Donna's devastation in 1960 forced her to leave. (Courtesy of the State Archives of Florida.)

Deaconess Harriet Bedell is seen above in front of the Glade Cross Mission sign in the mid-1950s. Bedell made it her life's mission to help the Indians become more self-reliant while reviving their doll-making and basket-weaving skills, which had nearly become extinct. She was basically acting as a nonprofit for the Indians. Below, Bedell and Mikasuki Indians stand by a car in the Everglades sometime during 1933–1960. (Both, courtesy of the State Archives of Florida.)

Deaconess Harriet Bedell is pictured at left with two local Indian women in Everglades around the early 1950s. Bedell knew that few Indians could read or write English and their children were not sent to white schools; that working with these Indians would be a tremendous task. Undaunted, Bedell persisted and, little by little, gained their trust. Bedell shared that one of the hardest parts of her duties was while completing her parish rounds when she would have to "pole" a dugout canoe through the swamps to reach those isolated Seminole Indians. Below is another view of Bedell's beloved Glade Cross Mission in Everglades City, Florida. Bedell made it possible for the Indians' handiwork to be put on display at the mission, including bead necklaces and bracelets, dolls, baskets, and clothing, which were all on sale. (Both, courtesy of the State Archives of Florida.)

Mama Hokie, seen at right, lived along the Tamiami Trail in Ochopee, Florida, and faced death twice head-on—and lived to tell it both times. Her first encounter was with an alligator who ended up taking off her right forearm after she walked out onto her wooden bridge. She survived following several months of rehab. Her second near-fatal encounter came following Tropical Depression Jerry in 1996. After the water rose over the canals, it came rushing into her home, and she fell while praying to be rescued. She was rescued; however, the incident left her weak, which turned into pneumonia and then her passing in December 1996. The former cryptic sign below, viewed along the Tamiami Trail near the vicinity of the smallest post office, offered beer *and* worms. (Both, courtesy of Lila Zuck.)

While Jimmie House Robinson is no longer with us, the local fishermen and women are grateful for her dedication and hard work that has enabled the Organized Fishermen of Florida (OFF) to remain a viable entity even today, some 50 years later. (Courtesy of Jeanie Smith.)

Paolita way station mistress Elva McGill is shown at right behind the way station, next to a young deer she had just shot and killed. When McGill passed at age 71, her pallbearers were a veritable who's who from the local community, including Preston Sawyer, Meece Ellis Jr., Alto Griffin, and Stanley Whidden. The below aerial shot of the Paolita way station was taken during the early 1930s, shortly after the completion of both the Tamiami Trail and the six way stations. It also shows the Miccosukee Indian village directly across the street. (Both, courtesy of Lynda Lee Little.)

Deputy Blanche Maynard was known to thwart a few minor squabbles around town while maintaining the peace as well as law and order. She was respectfully known as a "tough old bird." In this photograph are, from left to right, Elsie Bothelho Maynard, William Riley Maynard (the grown-up two-year-old son discussed in her former deputy days), Deputy Maynard, and former sheriff W.R. Maynard. (Courtesy of Wayne Maynard.)

Six
HISTORICALLY SIGNIFICANT

Since the beginning of time, hurricanes have been an important part of the Everglades' history. The first recorded hurricane to directly hit the Everglades happened on September 18, 1926. Names for hurricanes were not added until 1953, but this hurricane was significant due in part to the fact that the Tamiami Trail was currently under construction at the time the hurricane hit. And in its wake, it left behind not just feet of water, but it also destroyed bridges and bits of roadway that had just been completed.

The next major hurricane to disrupt Southwest Florida was on September 10, 1960, when Hurricane Donna bore down on the tiny town of Everglades City, leaving it completely inundated with eight feet of water.

The town of Everglades City came out to witness the opening and dedication services of the Everglades National Park on December 6, 1947. With Pres. Harry S. Truman on the dais, proclaiming, "Here are no lofty peaks seeking the sky, no mighty glaciers or rushing streams wearing away the uplifted hand. Here is land, tranquil in its quiet beauty, serving not as the source of water but as the last receiver of it." Following the dedication ceremony, guests were treated to a specially made, Florida-shaped baked cake, overseen by Everglades Inn chef Claus "Snooky" Senghaas.

For nearly 50 years, beginning in 1973, Everglades City has held an annual seafood festival as a town fundraiser on the second weekend in February. The normal 500-resident population swells to many thousands during this one weekend as it makes money for the local schoolchildren and much-needed community projects. The first festival was held to raise money for much-needed playground equipment. On that very first festival, the locals were expecting to feed roughly 500 people and were shocked to learn that over 5,000 people were in attendance, creating the very first traffic jam in Everglades City.

The unnamed 1926 hurricane that battered tiny Everglades left lots of flooding behind after hitting nearby Miami. The photograph above shows West Broadway inundated with water. For identification purposes, the two-story white building in the center of the image was the town's first jail. The image below depicts the raging waters in front of the Everglades Club. (Both, courtesy of the State Archives of Florida.)

Hurricane Donna scored a direct hit on Everglades City, Naples, and Marco Island on September 10, 1960, with its 110-mile-per-hour winds, leaving the city inundated with eight feet of water. The photograph above shows the destruction Donna created inside the Glade Cross Mission in Everglades City. It was so destructive that it left Deaconess Harriet Bedell homeless. The photograph below shows the flooding along a residential street in Everglades City following Donna in 1960. (Both, courtesy of the State Archives of Florida.)

Pres. Harry S. Truman, seen above at the podium, dedicates the Everglades National Park on December 6, 1947, to a jubilant crowd of over 5,000, pictured below, in Everglades. This 28th national park was different from most. It was established as a park not because of its spectacular scenery, but to protect its very delicate environment. It took several decades before Congress approved the plans in 1934. Without realizing the environmental importance this slow-moving water provided to the health and welfare of the state, engineers began "draining the swamps" beginning in 1906, to create dairy farms and vegetable fields. Sadly, their dredging, diking, and canal building continued for the next two decades, destroying thousands of years of natural evolution. It is the only subtropical wilderness preserve in the United States. (Both, courtesy of the State Archives of Florida.)

The primitive chickee hut entrance booth (above) at the Everglades National Park, located at Long Key, was built in keeping with both the Miccosukee and Seminole traditions when the park opened in 1947. The United Nations declared the Everglades National Park an International Biosphere Reserve in 1976; three years later, a World Heritage Site; and in 1987, a Wilderness of International Significance. The main park road into the Everglades National Park runs 38 miles from the Homestead Florida City entrance southwest to Flamingo. Both plant and animal life in this subtropical Everglades is a unique blend of species, due in part to heavy seasonal rainfall and tropical temperatures. This park map below is from around 1950. The park is open 365 days, including holidays. (Both, courtesy of the State Archives of Florida.)

Former Florida senator Claude Pepper wrote postmaster general Robert Emmet Hannegan on July 9, 1947, petitioning for a postage stamp to commemorate the upcoming dedication of the Everglades National Park. The unveiling of this Everglades National Park 3¢ commemorative postage stamp was held on December 5, 1947, and 122,362,000 stamps were issued. The green stamp at left, designed by Miami graphic artist Garnett W. Megee, was one of the best-selling stamps in the history of the US Postal Service. It features a great white heron in the foreground, with a map of Florida in the background, while highlighting the Everglades National Park at the southern tip of the Florida peninsula. The first-day issue of the Everglades National Park stamp and envelope can be seen in the photograph below. (Left, courtesy of the State Archives of Florida; below, author's collection.)

88

Snooky Senghaas oversees the icing of the specially baked Florida-shaped cake, along with an unidentified pastry chef and assistant, prior to its presentation following the Everglades National Park's dedication on December 6, 1947, in Everglades. (Courtesy of HistoryMiami Museum.)

Attendees at the annual Everglades City Seafood Festival can expect to find fish chowder, stone crab claws, shrimp, and fried mullet, along with the usual sides of hush puppies, coleslaw, and even smoked mullet. Traditional Indian fry bread and burgers are also included on the menu. This aerial shot of the 1994 seafood festival offers a bird's-eye view of the hundreds of attendees. (Photograph by author.)

Seven
NEIGHBORING CHOKOLOSKEE ISLAND

Chokoloskee, a Seminole Indian word meaning "old house," can be found at the lower end of Collier County. The island was an important Indian habitation long before either the Seminoles or white man discovered it. John Weeks is recorded to have been the first settler of record on the island but was not fond of the isolation, and he persuaded Adolphus Santini to join him by giving him half of the island, according to historian Charlton W. Tebeau. Charles Greenleigh "C.G." McKinney would arrive next to this area in 1886 and rename the island Comfort. It seems settlers came, stayed briefly, and then moved on.

McKinney would have been the closest thing to a doctor since he was a practicing midwife and, while living in Texas after the Civil War, had learned the basics of dentistry. He was also instrumental in obtaining the first post office south of Fort Myers, established on November 27, 1891. The name "Comfort" only lasted a few months and was followed by present-day Chokoloskee.

C.S. "Ted" Smallwood, who arrived in 1887 and established his own trading post, complete with post office, would become postmaster in 1906 and would hold that position for the next 35 years. Smallwood traded with the local Seminole and Miccosukee Indians. The Indians would bring in animal hides, produce, and fish to trade for other goods until the Tamiami Trail opened in 1928.

Residents here were isolated from the town of Everglade, later known as Everglades and then Everglades City, until 1956, when the causeway was completed. Until then, all traffic was by boat; even students went to school in nearby Everglade by boat.

In 1913, the Chokoloskee Church of God was established, with land donated by C.G. McKinney. Sadly, the original church was destroyed by a hurricane and later replaced with another wooden structure. And with various seasonal hurricanes and no-name storms hitting the island over the past century blowing off this roof or that bell, it is surprising that it remains intact and is still serving the island parishioners today.

This is an aerial shot of Chokoloskee Island, Florida, taken in 1994, nearly 40 years after the causeway connected it to the Everglades City mainland. Roughly 400 people were counted as residents for the 2000 census, and the numbers are much the same as of this writing. (Photograph by author.)

C.G. McKinney (1847–1926) was known as the man who put the "chuckle" in Chokoloskee with his humorous depictions of bootleggers, swamp angels (mosquitoes), preachers, and backsliders in his columns for the former weekly *American Eagle* newspaper in Estero, Florida. Everything was fair game to write about. A sample of some of his quips and comments are shown on the following page. (Courtesy of Lila Zuck.)

CHOKOLOSKEE

Chokoloskee, Fla., May 27, 1922.

We have had warm weather with cool nights and plenty of light showers this week. We find that the swamp angels are very backward. We are agreeably disappointed by their not appearing in great quantities, but we will raise no kick with them for their tardiness.

Our little scrap did not get in The Eagle last week, there were so many political seekers down at the mourners' bench praying to have consideration when it came time to skim the political pot. There will be a lot of them skimmed off the top of the pot and cast overboard, while there will be a few that will be fortunate or unfortunate enough to get their feet under the pie counter.

We have had a few Indians with us this week with alligator skins.

The Ethel Q. was down again last Monday with a few groceries for the folks.

There is not much doing in the fish business now,—too many stops, wait awhile, etc. We hear of another fish company buying out the South Fish Company. If they make the deal we hope it will be for the better or worse.
PROGRESS.

A vote for H. A. Hendry for Representative is a vote against County Division!

CHOKOLOSKEE

Chokoloskee, Fla., June 17, 1922.

We have had warm and rainy weather this week; mercury up to 91° and the swamp angels up to about the limit for quantity, and they are mad.

We have seen something less than a dozen airmen sailing over the island this week.

We have had only a few Indians.

It appears that this has been a fighting week with us among the drunken team. One of the creatures got his face bruised up from meeting a board right square in his face.. We have no one to protect us. Our neck of the woods has been cast on the junk pile. It appears that the officials don't want to tackle it.

Messrs. Will Thompson and Miner Johnson have finished up Mr. C. G. McKinney's new store, except some inside work, and departed today for their home at Naples.

Moonshining is on the boom. A very suspicious looking thing came on the Ethel Q this week. We were told it was a still.
Progress.

CHOKOLOSKEE

[The following items were mailed us from Everglades post office by C. G. McKinney ("Progress") on Saturday, the morning of his death, these probably being the last lines penned by our venerable and much lamented Chokoloskee correspondent.—Editor's note.]

Chokoloskee, Fla., Oct. 16, 1926.

We are blessed with fine weather with some appearance of fall. We have very few swamp angels now.

Mercury has been acting like this: Last Saturday just before sunrise, 74; at 2 p. m., 85. Sunday, 75; at 2 p. m., 86. Monday, 74; at 2 p. m., 86. Tuesday, 75; at 2 p. m., 90. Wednesday, 78; at 2 p. m., 88. Thursday, 78; at 2 p. m., 85. Friday, 78; at 2 p. m., 87. Saturday (today), 77.

Mr. Nelson Noble is on the sick list and has gone up the coast for treatment.

Our work of overhauling wreckage is still going on. It is a mess and we hope the Good Lord will not give us such a dose soon again.

Fishing is fairly good.

Our peach tree got badly done up in the storm, but now it is putting out new leaves like spring time.

Mr. St. Clair Demere has moved from this island to Fakahatchee Island

Pictured are three random copies of Chokoloskee resident C.G. McKinney's column written for the *American Eagle* newspaper in Estero, Florida, in the 1920s. McKinney wrote about daily happenings on the isolated island. He wrote under both Sage and Progress as his bylines. (Courtesy of Collier County Museum.)

C.G. McKinney unexpectedly passed on October 16, 1926, in Everglades. His daughter Willie Corrinne McKinney penned these last words upon his death: "He was only an aged and obscure storekeeper on an unknown village on the edge of the Everglades, yet thousands who have read his unique reports and observations will feel a pang of sorrow at his death." (Photograph by author.)

Despite having only a third grade education, trading post proprietor Ted Smallwood (pictured at left) was quick to turn his trading post into the center of community activity, while cultivating a cultural bridge between the Indians and the white man, after learning their language. He was also blessed with a photographic memory and was so trusted by the Indians that he kept their money for them at his trading post. The photograph below shows the store Smallwood built on ground level. Smallwood would later raise the store on pilings in 1925 to prevent future flooding. (Left, courtesy of the State Archives of Florida; below, courtesy of Glenda Hancock.)

The photograph at right was taken of the raised trading post on Chokoloskee Island in 1925. A life-sized replica of owner Ted Smallwood, seen below, still watches fondly over his trading post, flyswatter in hand. Visitors can view the original ledgers from over the years where the daily transactions were logged. The trading post was added to the National Register of Historic Places in 1974. (Right, courtesy of Glenda Hancock; below, photograph by author.)

The Smallwood Trading Post remained open and in use until 1982. Smallwood's granddaughter would reopen the post in 1990, with 90 percent of the original goods inside still intact. Today, the trading post and museum serves as the perfect time capsule of Florida pioneer history here in the Ten Thousand Islands. These interior photographs, taken in 1994, show the various goods on hand, including numerous jars and a colorful Indian jacket, inside the Smallwood Trading Post. Today, in addition to various books, including those by local authors, Indian dolls and clothing, small toys, and T-shirts can also be purchased. (Both, photograph by author.)

The photograph above shows the exterior of the Smallwood Trading Post on Chokoloskee Island, Florida, during the 1950s. Note the post office sign over the front door. The photograph below shows the interior of the trading post and the window to the on-site post office with daughter Thelma Smallwood at the window in the early 1970s. (Both, courtesy of the State Archives of Florida.)

Pictured here in 1994 is the exterior of the Smallwood Trading Post, coupled with the addition of a wooden totem pole to the left of the stairs. The trading post has survived many storms and hurricanes over the years after having been raised on pilings in 1925. (Photograph by author.)

The above photograph of the Church of God, located on Chokoloskee Island, Florida, was taken in 1953, along with its parsonage, seen below, during its 40th anniversary. The Church of God was established in 1913. The original church was replaced in 1961 with the present concrete building. In 2005, when Hurricane Wilma hit the area with its 131-mile-per-hour winds, the church steeple was blown off and discovered approximately two blocks away during the cleanup effort. (Both, courtesy of Glenda Hancock.)

This is a c. 1970s photograph of the Church of God on Chokoloskee Island, Florida. The church held an all-day celebration on its centennial birthday in 2013, with current members comprised of former generations dating back to 1913. (Courtesy of Glenda Hancock.)

Local records show that the land underneath the former J.T.'s store (above) on Chokoloskee Island, Florida, once belonged to C.G. McKinney, who ran his own store in the late 1880s. However, there was a proprietor by the name of Brown who came to the Everglade, which most of this area was called back in the early 1900s, and opened his own store, shown in the 1913 photograph below. This current historical building began as a small corporate office in Everglade, Florida, behind the present-day Rod & Gun Club. After the causeway was completed in 1956, the building was moved by barge to Chokoloskee, Florida, and has been recycled numerous times over the years. (Both, courtesy of the State Archives of Florida.)

Seen here are two images of the former school boat, built by local native A.C. Hancock in 1953, after the Collier County School Board decided to combine the Everglades City School and the Chokoloskee School. Hancock was awarded the contract, and it took him three months to complete. The photograph above shows the school boat outside the Smallwood Trading Post. The image below shows the school boat out on the waterways. Students from the 5th through 12th grades would ride the boat for the next three years until the causeway was built and completed in 1956. The interior of the boat had a bench on each side of the craft with a table in the middle, and the exterior was painted white. Gus Rewis served as the school boat captain. (Both, courtesy of Glenda Hancock.)

Eight
The Town of Ochopee

With the completion of the Tamiami Trail by county namesake Barron Gift Collier in 1928, this former "Last Frontier" was now open for development. Within a few short years, Ochopee, a Seminole Indian word meaning "big field," boasted a three-story boardinghouse with its own café, general store, and post office; a packinghouse; a garage; and more. Ochopee was considered the halfway point between Fort Myers and Miami, and once the trail was open, travelers began stopping.

Prior to being called Ochopee, the area was known as Gaunt's Place, after tomato farmer James T. Gaunt, and from 1928 through 1953 "tomatoes were king." Unfortunately, on May 12, 1953, while at the three-story boardinghouse, a transient truck driver had returned to his rented room following his supper at the café. He had been drinking and smoking and apparently passed out because the next thing anyone knew, the building was on fire. The truck driver died from his injuries the following day. While waiting for the nearest fire department to respond, the residents were filling their buckets from the local canal. Unfortunately, the fire truck's hoses broke, and everyone had to just stand back and watch it burn to the ground. It was sad to watch one building igniting the next and then the next. Fortunately, postmaster Sidney Brown was able to save his postal records.

Raymond Wooten and his family would literally stumble upon a new way to show tourists the area by water—in a frog boat (airboat)—and in 1953, Wooten's Everglades Airboat Tours in Ochopee, Florida, opened. Wooten made more money providing tours than he did working at the local garage, so he bought a few acres of local swampland and soon began his business, which still thrives today.

Continuing along on the Tamiami Trail toward Miami was the former Golden Lion Motor Inn, which originally opened on Christmas 1970 after the Whichello siblings had pooled their inheritance monies together to open their dream project. But their dream soon soured when the National Park Service came knocking on their door.

Above, postmaster Sidney Brown stands in front of the world's smallest post office during the mid-1950s, in Ochopee, Florida, near Carnestown. Who knew that this makeshift post office, and former irrigation shed, measuring eight feet, four inches by seven feet, three inches, would stand the test of time, and several hurricanes too, while becoming a national landmark and tourist attraction? On March 21, 1962, a special 60th anniversary celebration was held on behalf of the smallest post office in the world, in Ochopee, Florida. The US postal authorities even marked the occasion with a special commemorative envelope, seen below. (Above, courtesy of the State Archives of Florida; below, author's collection.)

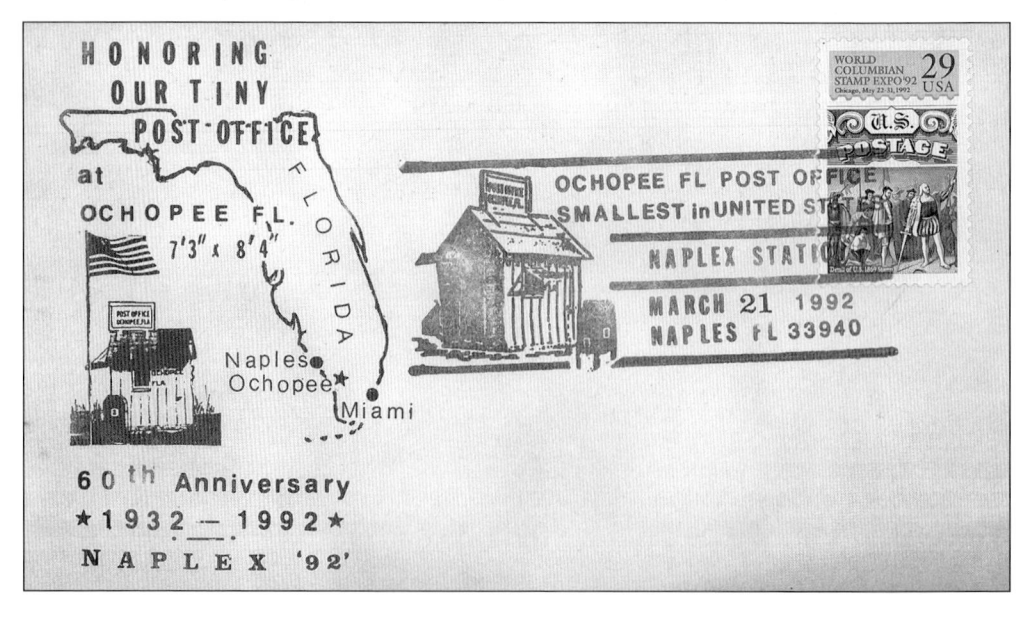

This is an early 1970s image of Wooten's Everglades Airboat Tours with founder Raymond himself at the wheel. Raymond's son Gene, who had inherited the 60-year-old family business initially begun in 1953, sold the business in late 2013. Wooten's still offers exciting rides for people of all ages through its 259 private acreage. The company's tagline reads: "Showing the REAL Everglades since 1953." (Courtesy of State Archives of Florida.)

Above, this advertising postcard promotes the spacious rooms, restaurant, and pool at the Golden Lion Motor Inn, formerly owned by the Whichello families, located in Ochopee, Florida, along the Tamiami Trail. The family's great American dream of owning its own business was soon thwarted in order for the National Park Service to establish the Big Cypress National Preserve. Today, the former motor inn serves as the headquarters offices for the Big Cypress National Preserve. When the motor inn opened in December 1970, the pool, shown below, was an immediate hit with the local children in the area since the closest pool at that time was seven miles away in Everglades City. (Both, courtesy of the Jeff Whichello family.)

This is an aerial shot of the former Golden Lion Motor Inn, located along the Tamiami Trail in Ochopee, Florida, that once belonged to members of the Whichello family. Jeff Whichello, who grew up in the four-square-mile "heart" of Ochopee, has written a book called *What Happened to Ochopee?*, recounting his family's struggle and those of their neighbors. (Courtesy of the Jeff Whichello family.)

In Carnestown, Florida, a workman pushes a loaded handcart of freshly picked tomatoes from Gaunt's farms in nearby Ochopee into a railroad boxcar for shipment. The loading dock and packinghouse are behind him to the right. The original handwritten caption for this c. 1950s image reads, "Loading House." (Courtesy of Collier County Museum.)

Nine

Visiting Copeland, Deep Lake, and Lee Cypress

Located along State Road 29, near today's Everglades City, was a former property known as the Copeland Road Prison, which was purchased by founder Barron Gift Collier in 1921. The Department of Corrections records show the prison opened in 1952 at a cost of $85,000. Records also indicate that it initially served as a maximum security prison, housing hardened criminals until 1960, following Hurricane Donna's direct hit on Everglades City. After the massive cleanup, all incoming prisoners were changed to those of a lower security. The prison permanently closed in 2002.

Across from the former prison was a small town called Deep Lake, with only a handful of residents, that was located along the defunct Atlantic Coast Railroad at State Road 29 (before Collier's arrival). Friends and partners John M. Roach and Walter Langford planted a grove of 12,000 Marsh-brand seedless grapefruit trees around 1901. They eventually built a railroad tram system, extending to Everglade, in order to retrieve and transport their grapefruit. Company records showed they shipped 17,000 boxes of Deep Lake grapefruit to market by 1915.

Doug McGoon, a community leader in the town of Lee-Cypress, built a church for the black community in the early 1940s. These were the same people who were working in the nearby logging camps. It was named Bula Missionary Baptist Church Mission and had a lengthy history over the years. Following its closure during integration, it was donated to local Lee-Cypress resident Frances Hodge. Hodge dedicated the old church to the community to be used as a meeting place in 2002, but it needed many repairs. It was sadly demolished on November 21, 2011, and the land was later sold in 2015.

From 1944 through 1957, the most extensive logging in Collier County was done by the Lee Tidewater Cypress Company in Copeland. During World War II, demand for the local and once plentiful, durable, rot-resistant cypress pushed loggers deeper into the 100-year-old forest to cut down the trees to be used for barrels, packing crates, and coffins.

Long-term inmates, before 1960, referred to the Copeland Road Prison as the "Alcatraz of the Everglades" and purposely escaped in order to be transferred elsewhere. The prison had a contract with the Department of Transportation to furnish 24 inmates each day to help with local road repairs or work at either the nearby state park or Everglades City. (Courtesy of Lila Zuck.)

The Copeland Road Prison was operational and at near capacity (76 inmates was the maximum allowed) in 1983, according to former captain H.L. Nolan. This tiny, well-kept chapel for the inmates' use, with the Reverend Clyde Martin providing Sunday services each week, was well maintained by the inmates. (Courtesy of Lila Zuck.)

Another of Barron Gift Collier's many industries was the seedless grapefruit grove he purchased from John M. Roach and Walter Langford in 1922. Collier revamped and renamed this industry the Collier County Canning Company (4-C), seen above. It was located in Deep Lake, where his own brand of grapefruit juice was made and then shipped north. A 4-C label is seen in the image below, showing the Marsh seedless grapefruit brand. Enter Florida-born and -raised Edmond F. Scott, the son of a citrus grower from Canada who began managing Collier's grapefruit grove and juice plant in 1929. Ever the marketing genius, Scott soon added a second shift to maintain the quotas. An interesting tidbit gleaned was that the Deep Lake Grapefruit brand was served at the Waldorf Astoria Hotel in New York City during the 1920s. (Both, courtesy of Collier County Museum.)

The small Bula Missionary Baptist Church Mission was donated to the black community of Lee-Cypress, Florida, in the early 1940s. In need of extensive repairs, including a new roof, local resident Frances Hodge donated it to the community for a meeting place in 2002. (Photograph by author.)

Collier County once had the largest remaining stands of virgin cypress as well as pine trees in the country, reaching upwards of 130 feet in some locations. From 1944 through the mid-1950s, Lee Tidewater Cypress Company was the largest cypress operation dedicated exclusively to logging cypress. Logging is extremely dangerous work, and the loggers worked long, grueling, 10–12 hour shifts they called "cain't see to cain't see," meaning they arrived before the sun rose and left long after the sun had set. This logging crew seen above around 1947 was ferried from the current Fakahatchee Strand locale over to Copeland on the local train. At right, Jimmy O'Connor is girdling this cypress tree in Copeland, draining the sap, which kills the tree, around 1948. (Above, courtesy of Collier County Museum; right, courtesy of the State Archives of Florida.)

In the photograph at left, a diesel-operated dragline machine is scooping up muck from the swamp bottom in Copeland, Florida, in order to make a dry grade for the railroad ties. In the c. 1948 photograph below, a train is pulling lumber from Copeland to be carried 15 miles into camp to be reloaded onto special railcars and then shipped 400 miles to the Perry Mill. (Both, courtesy of the State Archives of Florida.)

In this photograph, sawyers Rufus Beebe (left) and Norman Kimble (right) cut trees with a handsaw in Copeland, Florida, in 1948. Sawyers in three operating areas cut an average of 10,000 cypress feet per day. (Courtesy of the State Archives of Florida.)

Rufus Beebe files the saw's teeth to diamond-sharp points. These double-handle saws are filed once each day. This photograph was taken in 1948 in Copeland, Florida. (Courtesy of the State Archives of Florida.)

Flagman Willy Perry Jr., 19 years old, makes signals on a cypress stump. He signals the route of the log, warns loggers in the path of danger, and tells the skidder operator the position of the log in Copeland, Florida, in 1948. (Courtesy of the State Archives of Florida.)

Some of those "Giants of the Swamp" could measure 25 feet in circumference and reach heights of 130–150 feet. The company towns of Copeland and Jerome were the primary logging operations devoted to cutting cypress. The ultimate threat, loggers said, was being caught beneath a falling "Giant of the Swamp." (Courtesy of the State Archives of Florida.)

The photograph above shows the Lee Tidewater Cypress Company engine No. 4 stationed in Copeland, Florida. The below c. mid-1940s photograph shows a log train carrying cypress to Lee Cypress. By the winter of 1956–1957, all the economically harvested stands of cypress had been depleted, and the logging ceased. (Both, courtesy of the State Archives of Florida.)

123

Today, this Lee Tidewater Cypress Company engine No. 2 stands proudly behind the Collier County Museum headquarters, near the Collier County government center in Naples, for all to see. This steam engine was one of four engines on hand that were perfectly suited to the logging demands in the swamp. (Courtesy of the State Archives of Florida.)

Ten

A Giant Passes

While staying at his winter home on Useppa Island, Florida, in 1939, Barron Gift Collier fell ill and was so sick, he was taken to a hospital in New York. Collier passed on March 13, 1939, just 10 days before his 66th birthday. His passing was carried by the Associated Press and many other newspapers throughout the country while public tributes also poured in. Hundreds of people attended his funeral held three days later on March 16. Politicians, business colleagues, friends, family, and others attended in order to pay their respects. Collier was buried in historic Woodlawn Cemetery, New York, along with other family members.

Southwest Florida was his true passion, and Barron Gift Collier was indeed the "Gift" to Southwest Florida.

This Barron Gift Collier Monument and bust are located in Collier-Seminole State Park, just off the Tamiami Trail in Naples, Florida. Visitors to the park can see the historic Bay City walking dredge, used during construction of the Tamiami Trail. There is also a replica of a Seminole War–era Army blockhouse on the park grounds, built by the Civilian Conservation Corps (CCC) in the 1930s. (Courtesy of the State Archives of Florida.)

About the Author

Author Maureen Sullivan-Hartung was born in Huntington, West Virginia, and after residing in both Ohio and Kentucky, she moved to Naples, Florida, in the summer of 1981. For the first decade, she worked for two local interior designers before switching careers. In 1993, Sullivan-Hartung began reporting for the former weekly *Everglades Echo* newspaper. It was during this job that she met the late and colorful Chokoloskee resident Totch Brown, who took her out on his boat during her first interview with him and shared the local history of this area. Thus began her love affair with Collier County's early history. After freelance writing for numerous publications for the next seven years, Sullivan-Hartung decided to write her first book on Everglades City to capture as much history as possible before it was completely lost. *Hidden History of Everglades City & Points Nearby* was published in 2010 by The History Press. Her second book, Images of America: *Everglades City*, was published by Arcadia Publishing in 2020.

For additional information, including images and speaking engagement requests, please check her website at www.maureenwrites.com.

DISCOVER THOUSANDS OF LOCAL HISTORY BOOKS
FEATURING MILLIONS OF VINTAGE IMAGES

Arcadia Publishing, the leading local history publisher in the United States, is committed to making history accessible and meaningful through publishing books that celebrate and preserve the heritage of America's people and places.

Find more books like this at
www.arcadiapublishing.com

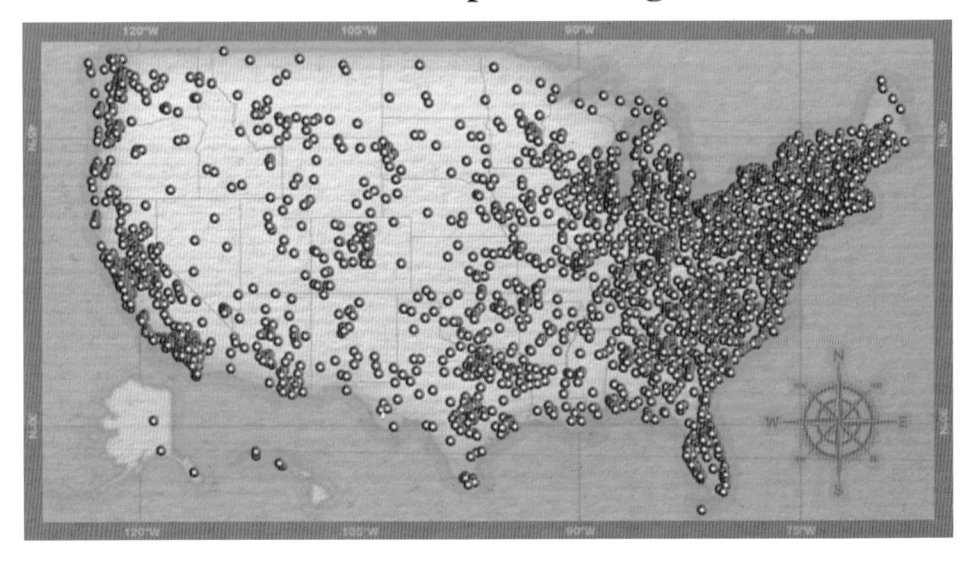

Search for your hometown history, your old stomping grounds, and even your favorite sports team.

Consistent with our mission to preserve history on a local level, this book was printed in South Carolina on American-made paper and manufactured entirely in the United States. Products carrying the accredited Forest Stewardship Council (FSC) label are printed on 100 percent FSC-certified paper.

MADE IN THE USA